UK DVSA MOTORCYCLIST THEORY TEST

Over 200 motorcycle theory test/exams questions and answers extracted from DVSA Highway Code question bank

Theodore. G. Armstrong

Copyright

Table of Contents

Introduction

Every motorcyclist must have adequate information and theoretical knowledge of driving before proceeding to the road for the real driving experience.

This book will give you all the theoretical lessons you need to nail your written exams. The first information you need to have is that there no need for anxiety.

Potential drivers need to know what to expect in their DSVA motorcyclists theory test so that they can be well prepared.

Questions from this book are extracted right out of the official Highway Code to help you prepare for the exams to avoid loss of time, energy, and money.

Study the material many times for proper absorption of the content therein.

Enjoy your ride.

Chapter 1

Theory Test 1

1. **Your rear wheel skids as you accelerate while riding in heavy rain. To regain control of your ride, what must you do?**

   a) Change down to a lower gear.

   b) Put your feet down

   c) Ease off the throttle

   d) Brake to reduce speed

2. **When you are carrying a heavy road on your motorcycle, you may need to adjust one of the following.**

   a) The tyre pressure

   b) The gear lever

   c) The footrests

   d) The seat height

3. **What does this sign mean?**

   a) No parking for solo motorcycles

   b) Parking for solo motorcycles

   c) Parking for police motorcycles

d) Passing place for motorcycles

4. **What information can you see on a vehicle registration document?**

   a) The security number of the ignition-key

   b) The original purchase price

   c) The service history

   d) The make and model

5. **One of the following methods of fastening helmet is unsafe?**

   a) Double D-ring fastening

   b) Quick-release fastening

   c) Velcro tab

   d) Bar and buckle

6. **You're on a motorway riding. Suddenly a car in front, while still in motion, switches on its hazard warning lights. What does this mean?**

   a) It means there's danger ahead.

   b) The driver is trying to maneuver lanes.

   c) There's an oncoming police car.

   d) The driver will exit at the junction.

7. **What information can you see on a motorcycle's registration document?**

   a) The registered keeper's name

   b) The type of insurance cover required

   c) The service history

   d) The date of the MOT

8. **The day is very sunny, and your indicators are difficult to see. To let other road users know your intention, what should you do?**

   a) Flash your headlights.

   b) Keep both hands on the handlebars.

   c) Sound your horn.

   d) Give an arm signal.

9. **There is a strong side wind, and you are riding on a long open motorway. In which of the following situation are you going to be extra careful?**

   a) When there is a slow movement of traffic.

   b) When you are approaching an exit or a slip road.

   c) When you overtake a large vehicle.

   d) When you are approaching a service area.

10. **Why should a motorcyclist avoid riding over this marked area?**

   a) They might be patches of oil left by a bus.

   b) It's illegal to ride over bus stops.

   c) Pedestrians may at the bus stop.

d) The centre of gravity of your vehicle might change.

11. **You're about to turn right at a large roundabout to cross a lane to reach your exist. What should you do?**

a) Look over your left shoulder.

b) Put on your right indicator.

c) Cancel the left indicator.

d) Look over your right shoulder.

12. **What does 'tailgating' mean?**

a) When you follow another vehicle too closely.

b) When you drive with rear fog lights on.

c) When you use the rear door of a hatchback car.

d) When you reverse into a parking space.

13. **'Red routes' is introduced in major cities because?**

a) It helps Lorries to load more freely.

b) It helps raise the speed limits.

c) It provides better parking.

d) It helps the traffic flow.

14. **What methods will a school crossing patrol use to signal you to stop?**

a) By displaying a 'stop' sign

b) By displaying a red light

c) By shouting at the passerby

d) By giving you an arm signal

15. Where would you see this sign display?

 a) At the edge of the road

 b) On the rear of a coach or school bus

 c) At children's playground areas

 d) In a private car's window with children inside.

16. There is a slow-moving motorcyclist on a motorway. And you are about to overtake it, which of the following sign would make you take extra care?

a)

b)

c)

d)

17. **You want to emerge left from a minor road and found out that a large vehicle is approaching from the right. Why should you wait when you have time to turn?**

a) The large vehicle can easily cover vehicles coming from the left.

b) The large vehicle can easily cover an overtaking vehicle.

c) The large vehicle finds it difficult to steer in a straight line.

d) The large vehicle can turn suddenly.

18. **What is usually the speed limit of a road with street lights but no speed-limit signs?**

a) 30 mph

b) 60 mph

c) 40 mph

d) 50 mph

19. **Which of the following road users can use a toucan crossing?**

a) Buses and Lorries

b) Cars and motorcycles

c) Cyclists and pedestrians

d) Trams and trains

20. **Which sign indicates pedestrians walking along the road?**

a)

b)

c)

d)

21. **What does a red traffic light mean?**

a) Proceed with care

b) Ignore and speed off

c)   Stop and wait behind the stop line

d)   Stop unless you are turning left

22. **It's important to check your tyre pressures regularly. When is the right time to check your tyre pressure?**

a)   After a long journey

b)   When tyres are hot

c)   After riding at high speed

d)   When tyres are cold

23. **Two cyclists are riding in front of you. They came to a roundabout in the left-hand lane. Which direction will the cyclists go?**

a)   Right

b)   Any direction

c)   Straight ahead

d)   Left

24. **When you see this sign at a crossroads, what does it mean?**

a)   Find another route

b)   Maintain the same speed

c)   Carry on with great care

d) Telephone the police

25. **You're following a cyclist and want to turn left, what should you do?**

    a) Move around the cyclist on the junction.

    b) Pull alongside and stay at the same level as the cyclists until after the junction.

    c) Hold back and allow the cyclist to pass the junction.

    d) Speed up and overtake the cyclist before you reach the junction.

26. **In a two-lane dual carriageway. What will you use the right-hand lane use for?**

    a) To overtake slower traffic.

    b) To maintain a constant speed limit..

    c) To maintain the minimum carriageway speed.

    d) For normal progress.

27. **Which color follows the green light at a puffin crossing?**

    a) Flashing amber

    b) Steady amber

    c) Flashing green

    d) Steady red

28. **On which type of vehicle will you find this yellow sign displayed?**

a) A broken-down vehicle

b) An ice-cream van

c) A school bus

d) A private ambulance

29. **When are you permitted to overtake on the left while travelling along a motorway?**

   a) When you warn other road users behind by signalling left.

   b) When you can see ahead clearly.

   c) When you are in queues and traffic to your right is moving more slowly than you are.

   d) When the right-hand lane traffic is moving right.

30. **What's the national speed limit for a motorcycle or car on a motorway unless stated otherwise?**

   a) 70 mph

   b) 50 mph

   c) 60 mph

   d) 80 mph

31. **Which of the following road users are allowed to use toucan crossings?**

   a) Motorcyclists and pedestrians

b) Only cyclists

c) Cyclists and pedestrians

d) Motorcyclists and cyclists

32. What does the MOT certificate enable you to do?

a) To tax your vehicle.

b) To change your insurance company.

c) To renew your driving licence.

d) To notify a change of address.

33. A driver is suffering from shock as a result of a collision. What should you do?

a) Reassure them

b) Give them a drink

c) Give them food

d) Ask who is at fault

34. What should be the first thing to do when you just arrived at the scene of a motorcycle crash? No other road user was involved and you found the rider lying in the middle of the road unconsciously.

a) Clear the road of debris.

b) Warn other traffic.

c) Move the rider out of the road.

d) Reassure the rider

35. **Moving off from a parked position requires extra care. How should you move off safe and sound from a parked position?**

   a) Leave your motorcycle where it is parked until the road is clear.

   b) Use your indicator and also a hand signal.

   c) Signal other drivers slow down.

   d) Look over your shoulder for the last check.

36. **To prevent a cable-operated clutch from becoming stiff, what should you do?**

   a) Keep the cable oiled

   b) Keep the cable dry

   c) Keep the cable slack

   d) Keep the cable tight

37. **What causes tyres to lose their grip on the road surface and skid?**

   a) Giving hand signals

   b) Looking over your shoulder

   c) Heavy braking

   d) Riding one-handed

38. **Why is it important for a rider to make a lifesaver check before turning right?**

   a) To check if the rear indicator is flashing.

   b) To confirm the intention to turn.

   c) To check for any overtaking traffic.

   d) To ensure the side road is clear.

39. What do Traction control systems (TCS) fitted to some motorcycles help to prevent?

a) Uneven front tyre wear.

b) Skidding when braking too hard.

c) Uneven rear tyre wear.

d) Wheelspin when accelerating.

40. What does this sign mean?

a) End of clearway

b) End of a cycle route

c) End of restricted speed area.

d) End of the restricted parking area.

41. What does this sign mean?

a) Tall bridge

b) Road narrows

14

c) End of a narrow bridge.

d) End of dual carriageway.

42. What does this sign mean?

a) Divert at next exit

b) Hard shoulders are not allowed for lorries.

c) Lane for heavy and slow vehicles

d) Rest area for lorries

43. What does this sign mean?

a) Traffic lights out of order.

b) Red signal out of order.

c) New traffic lights ahead.

d) Temporary signal ahead.

44. You are riding and noticed horse riders in front. What should be your first reaction?

a) Accelerate around them

b) Signal right

c) Slow down and be ready to stop

d) Look for an alternative route.

45. **It can be beneficial to plan your route before starting a journey. Why is planning an alternative route also necessary?**

a) To make the journey easy.

b) To get held up by a tractor.

c) Your maps may have different scales.

d) In case the original route is blocked

46. **What does this sign mean?**

a) No pedestrians allowed.

b) Zebra crossing ahead.

c) Pedestrian zone - no vehicles.

d) School crossing patrol.

47. **You are driving on a motorway and intend to turn right at the end of the road. You noticed that some parked vehicles are blocking your view. What should you do next?**

a) Do nothing and wait.

b) Stop, and move forward slowly until you see clearly.

c) Do a U-turn and look for an exit.

d) Inquire from a pedestrian when to emerge.

48. **What does third-party insurance on your motorcycle cover?**

a) It covers cost in case of an accident

b) Loss of your motorcycle

c) Damaged cost by an accident

d) None of the above.

49. **When should you rest when riding on a long journey**

a) Once in a year

b) At the end of the journey

c) Every four hours

d) Every two hours

50. **Safety is important to stay alive. What can you do as a motorcycle rider to improve your safety on the road?**

a) Learn to ride faster.

b) Always ride at the centre of the road

c) Anticipate the intention of other road users.

d) Always ride near the kerb.

Answers To Theory Test 1

1	2	3	4	5	6	7	8	9	10
C	A	A	D	C	A	A	D	C	A

11	12	13	14	15	16	17	18	19	20
A	A	D	A	B	C	B	A	C	B

21	22	23	24	25	26	27	28	29	30
C	D	B	C	C	A	B	C	C	A

31	32	33	34	35	36	37	38	39	40
C	A	A	B	D	A	C	C	D	D

41	42	43	44	45	46	47	48	49	50
D	C	A	C	D	B	B	D	D	C

Chapter 2

Theory Test 2

1. **The work of the Reflective studs on the road helps you judge your position on the motorway at night or in poor visibility. Where are the reflective amber studs positioned on a motorway?**

   a) On the right-hand verge of the road.

   b) On the left-hand verge of the road.

   c) Separating the slip route from the motorway.

   d) Separating the carriageway lanes.

2. **As you are approaching the junction controlled by the traffic lights, you notice the amber traffic light ahead. Which light, or lights, will follow next?**

   a) Red alone

   b) Red and amber together

   c) Green and amber together

   d) Green alone

3. You're driving past queuing traffic and observe this road marking. What does it mean?

    a) Loading and off-loading point for Lorries.

    b) Slow down schoolchildren crossing.

    c) Pedestrians will be waiting in the road

    d) Traffic could be turning or emerging here

4. If you see an amber light at a pelican crossing flashing, what should you do?

    a) Allow the pedestrians already on the crossing to pass

    b) Ignore and continue with our driving

    c) Stop and wait for the red light

    d) Stop and wait for the green light

5. Motorcyclists are advised to wear bright clothing because?

    a) It helps them to stay safe

    b) It helps them to be warm

    c) It keeps them cool in the summer

    d) Drivers often do not see them

6. What does this sign mean?

a) Bridge over the road

b) Road ahead ends

c) Uneven road surface

d) Water across the road

7. **You were driving on a motorway and came across an inexperienced driver. What should you do?**

a) Sound your horn to scare them.

b) Be patient and be ready for them to react more slowly.

c) Flash your headlights and tell them to proceed.

d) Ignore and overtake.

8. **You at a scene of an incident, and someone is suffering from severe burns. What should you do?**

a) Douse the area affected by burns with clean, cool, and non-toxic liquid.

b) Remove anything that stock to the burns.

c) Apply moisturizing lotions to the injury.

d) Burst any blisters.

9. **What should you do, while you're waiting at a level crossing, a train passes, but you noticed that the lights are still flashing?**

   a) Park and investigate.

   b) Ignore the lights and move on.

   c) Phone the signal operator.

   d) Carry on waiting.

10. **After you've adjusted the tension on your drive chain, what next should you check?**

    a) Sidelights

    b) Tyre pressures

    c) Rear-wheel alignment

    d) Valve clearances

11. **In icy conditions, the tyre grip is greatly reduced. Your stopping distance will increase by how much in icy conditions?**

    a) Ten times

    b) Five times

    c) Three times

    d) Two times

12. **A top box is situated at the very back of the motorcycle. The item you should carry in your top box is:**

    a) Lightweight items

    b) Heavy items

    c) Personal items

d) Emergency items

13. **When you ride along a road where there are road humps, what should you do?**

    a) Keep a reduced speed all through

    b) Speed up quickly between each one

    c) Always maintain the maximum legal speed

    d) Ride slowly at school times only

14. **On what conditions are motorcyclists permitted to use a high-intensity rear fog light?**

    a) When riding a large touring machine.

    b) When carrying a pillion passenger.

    c) When they have visibility of 100 metres (328 feet) or less

    d) When riding on the road for the first time

15. **When you find yourself close to this lorry, what should you do?**

    a) Slow down and be ready to wait

    b) Signal the lorry wait for you

    c) Flash your lights at the lorry

    d) Drive your bike to the right-hand side of the road.

16. You're on a motorway. You observed that a lorry in front of you has stopped in the right-hand lane. And the sign below is displayed on the lorry. What must be your next action?

   a) Drive into the right-hand lane

   b) Stop behind the flashing lights

   c) Follow the next exit and leave the motorway.

   d) Pass the lorry on the left

17. The roads are wet after rain, and you are riding at night. The reflections from the road's surface are going to affect you in one of the following ways:

   a) To stop becomes easier.

   b) To accelerate becomes harder.

   c) To see unlit objects becomes easier.

   d) To see unlit objects becomes harder.

18. Overtaking a large vehicle is more difficult than overtaking a car. Why?

   a) The large vehicle does not move fast.

   b) A large vehicle is fitted with a speed limiter.

   c) Large vehicles have air brakes.

d) It will take a longer time to pass one.

19. **You're travelling behind a moped, and you want to turn left ahead. What should you do?**

a) Maintain your position until the moped has passed the junction.

b) Sound your horn and speed pass the moped.

c) Stop and wait for the moped to pass the junction.

d) Overtake the moped before the junction.

20. **What is the best position to stay while making use of the emergency telephone?**

a) Face the oncoming traffic

b) Stay close to the carriageway

c) Keep your back to the traffic

d) Stand on the hard shoulder

21. **When riding a motorcycle on a motorway, it is advisable to wear earplugs for one of the following reasons?**

a) To help prevent hearing damage

b) To make you less aware of traffic

c) To help keep you warm

d) To make your helmet fit better

22. **At a roundabout, which of the following vehicle is expected to take an unusual course?**

a) Estate car

b) Long lorry

c) Milk float

d) Delivery van

23. At the scene of an incident, a small child isn't breathing. How should you breathe into their mouth to restore normal breathing?

a) Heavily

b) Rapidly

c) Gently

d) Sharply

24. At a crossroads, you are turning right and an oncoming driver is also turning right. What action must you take?

a) Ensure the other vehicle stays to your left and turn in front of it (nearside to nearside)

b) Ensure the other vehicle stays to your right and turn behind it (offside to offside)

c) Ignore and turn at the next junction instead

d) Allow the other driver to turn first.

25. What does this sign mean?

a) Drive through the traffic

b) Right-hand lane T-junction only

c) Right-hand lane closed ahead

d) Left-hand lane closed ahead

26. **Which one of the following is the best place to park your motorcycle?**

a) On grass

b) On firm, level ground

c) On bumpy ground

d) On soft tarmac

27. **You came across an injured motorcyclist lying unconsciously in the road. The traffic has stopped, and there seems to be no danger. What should you do?**

a) Move the person off the road.

b) Remove their leather jacket.

c) Seek medical assistance.

d) Remove their safety helmet.

28. **Your motorcycle just broke down on the hard shoulder of a motorway. How do you rejoin the main carriageway when you have fixed the problem?**

a) Wait on the hard shoulder until other road users' flashes their headlights at you.

b) Don't wait; move onto the carriageway, and then build up your speed.

c) Use your hazard warning lights and move out onto the carriageway.

d) Build up sufficient speed on the hard shoulder, and then move out onto the carriageway

29. **You're driving through a long tunnel. How will you know if there is congestion or an incident ahead?**

a) Flashing lights coming from other road users

b) Hazard warning lines

c) Areas with hatch markings

d) Variable message signs

30. **While driving on a motorway, you see a road sign showing a sharp bend ahead. What should you do?**

a) Slow down before getting to the bend.

b) Slow down and reverse before the bend.

c) Slow down while coming out of the bend.

d) Ignore and continue at the same speed.

31. **When should you use a hard shoulder while on the motorway?**

a) In an emergency

b) When you want to answer a mobile phone.

c) When checking a road map.

d) When you are tired.

32. **What do yellow lines painted across the road mean?**

a) To tell you the distance to the roundabout

b) To make you aware of your speed and adjust where necessary

c) To help you follow the correct separation distance

d) To help you observe your front

33. **What is the effect of heavy braking and rapid acceleration on your vehicle?**

a) It increases fuel consumption

b) It increases road safety

c) It reduces pollution

d) It reduces exhaust emissions

34. **To carry a friend or a pillion passenger on your motorcycle, what condition must be met?**

a) You must possess a full motorcycle licence.

b) The pillion passenger must possess a full motorcycle licence.

c) You must possess 3years and above motorcycle riding experience.

d) You must have a big motorcycle

35. **When you are using a motorway, what basic rule applies?**

a) Overtake on the side that's free

b) Ride on the left-hand lane unless overtaking

c) Try to drive above 50 mph to avert congestion

d) Check the lane with the least traffic and use

36. **Why is it necessary to have mirrors fitted on each side of your motorcycle?**

    a)   To see the gap when filtering in traffic

    b)   To give protection when riding at night

    c)   To give the best view of the road behind

    d)   To avoid an accident

37. **You're riding at a speed of 70 mph on a three-lane motorway. Which lane should you use when there is no traffic ahead?**

    a)   The right-hand lane

    b)   The left-hand lane

    c)   The middle lane

    d)   Any lane

38. **There are no linked brakes on your motorcycle and you want to brake normally to stop. What should you do?**

    a)   Apply both brakes smoothly.

    b)   Apply only the rear brake

    c)   Apply only the front brake

    d)   Apply either of the brakes gently

39. **When you see a pedestrian at night putting on reflective clothing and holding a bright red light, what does it mean?**

    a)   It means you're approaching an organised walk.

    b)   It means you're approaching road works.

c) It means you're approaching a slow-moving vehicle.

d) It means you're approaching a traffic danger spot..

40. **What does Statutory Off-Road Notification (SORN) mean?**

   a) A way insurance companies check if a vehicle is insured.

   b) A notification to tell DVLA that a vehicle is no longer used on the road.

   c) Information by the police about the owner of a vehicle.

   d) A notification to tell DVSA of an accident.

41. **Why should you move towards the left side of the road when you are approaching a right-hand bend on your motorcycle?**

   a) To escape any slope or adverse curve.

   b) To have a better view of the road.

   c) To be on the safe side if your bike overturns.

   d) To be visible to oncoming traffic.

42. **A motorbike is travelling at 40 mph on a good road surface. The brakes and tyre are in excellent condition. The overall stopping distance for the motorbike is?**

   a) 174 feet (53 metres)

   b) 120 feet (36 metres)

c) 75 feet (23 metres)

d) 315 feet (96 metres)

43. **Horns are used only in exceptional cases; and you should use your motorcycle horn in which circumstances.**

a) To inform other road users of your presence.

b) To greet your friends.

c) To overtake a vehicle

d) To express that you have the right of way.

44. **Should you be worried if you notice oil on your front forks?**

a) No, only if the oil leak increases as you ride.

b) Yes, the oil could drip on the tyres causing loss of control.

c) Yes, the law is against riding with an oil leak.

d) No, there is nothing to worry about.

45. **Which of the following emergency vehicle has a flashing green light?**

a) Fire engine

b) Ambulance

c) Traffic enforcement officer's vehicle

d) Doctor's car

46. **In a motorway, the right-hand lane is only for what purpose?**

a) To overtake other vehicles

b) To slow down

c) For vehicles turning off at the next exit

d) For commercial vehicles only

47. **You noticed that it is snowing and you are about to travel. What should you do?**

a) Take a passenger with you.

b) Think about whether the journey is worth the risk.

c) Avoid a busy road, and follow a new route.

d) Keep yourself warm and continue with the journey.

48. **What should you check when a new rear wheel is fitted on your motorbike?**

a) The steering damper

b) The suspension

c) The tyre pressure

d) The wheel alignment

49. **When you negotiate a mini-roundabout, what should you avoid?**

a) Signalling too early

b) Lifesaver glances

c) Riding along the painted area

d) Right turns

50. **Which of the following vehicles cannot easily be affected by strong side winds.**

a) Motor cars

b) Cyclists

c) High-sided vehicles

d) Motorcycles

Answers To Theory Test 2

1	2	3	4	5	6	7	8	9	10
A	A	D	A	D	D	B	A	D	C

11	12	13	14	15	16	17	18	19	20
A	A	A	C	A	D	D	D	A	A

21	22	23	24	25	26	27	28	29	30
A	B	C	B	C	B	C	D	D	A

31	32	33	34	35	36	37	38	39	40
A	B	A	A	B	C	B	A	A	B

41	42	43	44	45	46	47	48	49	50
B	B	A	B	D	A	B	D	C	A

Chapter 3

Theory Test 3

1. **A clear helmet visor gives a good vision. You are riding along a country lane, and your helmet visor becomes fogged. What should you do?**

    a) Stop, park safely, and clean the visor.

    b) Stop and close the air vents on your helmet.

    c) Increase your speed to allow air to clean the visor.

    d) Ignore and continue riding until it clears.

2. **What is the difference between the toucan crossing and other crossings?**

    a) Cyclists use it.

    b) Mopeds use it.

    c) It has two flashing lights.

    d) A traffic officer controls it.

3. **Improper use of indicators can lead to road accidents. Why is it necessary to cancel the indicators after a manoeuvre?**

    a) To save battery.

    b) To avoid dazzling other traffic.

    c) To avoid damaging the indicator.

    d) To avoid confusing other road users.

4. **You are at a junction, and you see a rectangle with criss-cross yellow lines painted on the road. What does it indicate?**

   a) Left turns are permitted only.

   b) Stop at this position if the light changes.

   c) Do not block this area.

   d) The rectangle is a guide on the correct position to stay.

5. **Prohibitive signs that usually give orders look like what?**

   a) Blue circles

   b) Blue rectangles

   c) Red triangles

   d) Red circles

6. **Riding a motorcycle in cold weather might have which of the following effects on you?**

   a) You might feel more attentive.

   b) You might want to increase your speed.

   c) You might lose focus.

   d) You might feel comfortable and relaxed.

7. **You just fitted new tyres on your motorcycle. How are you going to ride it?**

   a) Brake hard into the bends to blend the new tyres.

   b) Increase the air pressure and ride normally.

   c) You have new tyres, so ride it quickly.

d) Be careful while riding it at first.

8. **What must you do before you come to a stop in normal conditions?**

   a) Put the motorcycle into neutral.

   b) Adjust the gear to first.

   c) Always use both mirrors before you decelerate

   d) Put both feet on the floor.

9. **What does a motorcycle catalytic converter do?**

   a) It helps to muffle exhaust noise

   b) It to reduce fuel consumption

   c) It helps to reduce noise pollution

   d) It helps to reduce exhaust emissions

10. **Lifesavers glance shows you what is hidden in the blind spots that your mirrors can't expose. When is the best time to take a lifesaver to check your blind spot?**

    a) Before moving off

    b) When speeding

    c) Before changing gears

    d) Before giving a signal

11. **How should you prevent a cable-operated clutch from becoming stiff in usage?**

    a) Slack.

    b) Dry and free from lubricants.

    c) Oiled.

    d) As tight as possible.

12. **When you see a driver in front rotates his or her right arm anticlockwise, this road signal indicates that:**
    a) The driver intends to turn left or move into the left
    b) The driver intends to stop or slow down
    c) The driver wants to turn right or move out to the right
    d) The driver wants you to pass his vehicle.

13. **How should you move when you are riding towards an unmarked crossroads?**
    a) Drive in the middle of the lane
    b) Keep right and slow down.
    c) Speed up as quickly as possible.
    d) Ride Slowly, look both ways and be ready to stop.

14. **The environmental factors that are likely to increase your stopping distance:**
    a) Nighttime
    b) Rain
    c) Strong winds
    d) Fog

15. **It's a good idea to plan your route before travelling. How can you achieve this?**
    a) Look at a map.
    b) Ask a friend.

c) Look at your licence.

d) Talk to your mechanic.

16. **You should avoid doing one of the following while riding at night:**

   a) Wear a tinted visor or glasses on your helmet.

   b) Use your headlight on full beam.

   c) Use your headlight with a dipped beam.

   d) Overtake other vehicles.

17. **The minimum legal tread depth for motorcycle tyres is:**

   a) mm

   b) 1.6 mm

   c) 4.0 mm

   d) 2.5 mm

18. **What does this sign mean?**

   a) Hump bridge

   b) Humps in the road

   c) Soft verges

   d) Entrance to tunnel

19. **What level should you fill your battery when you want to top it?**

a) Just below the cell plates

b) Halfway up the battery

c) The top of the battery

d) Just above the cell plates

20. **Unless otherwise stated, what's the national speed limit while riding on a motorway?**

a) 50 mph

b) 60 mph

c) 80 mph

d) 70 mph

21. **When you are riding your motorcycle, it is good to do regular lifesaver. The term "lifesaver" means?**

a) To take a glance over your shoulder before changing direction.

b) A motorcycle training certificate.

c) Insurance for motorcycle riders.

d) A special mirror that shows you what is in your blind spots.

22. **Your motorcycle oil light becomes illuminated while you are riding. What should you do?**

a) Stop and change the oil.

b) Stop as soon as you are safe to do so, and check the cause.

c) Ride with caution to avoid light disconnection.

d) Ride to the nearest garage and stop

23. **You are riding on a wet road and want to stop. The safest way to stop is to:**

    a)   Use the front brake only.

    b)   Use the rear brake only.

    c)   Use a lower gear only.

    d)   Use front and rear brakes simultaneously.

24. **What is the validity period of a Statutory Off-Road Notification (SORN)?**

    a)   It is valid until the vehicle is taxed, sold, or scrapped.

    b)   It is valid until the vehicle is used on the road.

    c)   It is valid until the vehicle is MOT'd and insured.

    d)   It is valid until the vehicle is modified or repaired.

25. **What is the typical overall stopping when you are ridding at 50 mph on a good dry road?**

    a)   36 metres (118 feet)

    b)   53 metres (175 feet)

    c)   75 metres (245 feet)

    d)   96 metres (315 feet)

26. **You came across zigzag lines on pedestrian crossings. What does it mean?**

a) No Sounding of horns at any time

b) Parking is not allowed at any time

c) Parking allowed

d) Slow down to 20 mph

27. The stability of your motorcycle is most likely to be reduced by one of the following road surfaces.

a) Concrete

b) Tarmac

c) Shellgrip

d) Loose gravel

28. What are the conditions required to tow a trailer with your motorcycle?

a) The trailer's width shouldn't be more than 1 metre (3 feet 3 inches).

b) The trailer should be equipped with brakes.

c) The weight of the trailer should be more than the motorcycle.

d) The motorcycle should have support coming from a sidecar.

29. **You are driving on a motorway. A red flashing light immediately appears above your lane only. What action should you take?**

   a) Ignore and continue riding on your lane

   b) Move into another lane when it is safe to do so.

   c) Ride on the hard shoulder.

   d) Stop and wait for instruction to continue.

30. **What does this sign mean?**

   a) Two-way traffic on a one-way road.

   b) Give priority to oncoming traffic.

   c) Two-way traffic straight ahead.

   d) One-way traffic crosses a two-way road.

31. **What do you see on the motorway on a very hot day?**

   a) Mud on the road

   b) A soft road surface

   c) Roadworks ahead

   d) Banks of fog

32. **You should be careful while riding on roads where electric trams operate because:**

a) They give off harmful emissions.

b) They brake very quickly.

c) They can't steer to dodge you.

d) They're slow movers.

33. **When you want to start a motorcycle engine, what safety measure should you take?**

a) Check that the neutral warning light is lit when the ignition is switched on.

b) Select first gear and, then apply the rear brake gently.

c) Select first gear and, then firmly apply the front brake.

d) Check that your taillights and dipped headlights are on.

34. **What is the use of a hard shoulder on a motorway?**

a) Stopping when you want to rest

b) Joining the motorway

c) Exiting the motorway

d) Stopping in an emergency

35. **The environmentally friendly vehicle is a vehicle powered by:**

a) Unleaded petrol

b) Electricity

c) Diesel

d) Gravity

36. **The left-hand lane on a three-lane motorway should be used by which type of vehicle?**

a) Slow vehicles only

b) Emergency vehicles only

c) Large vehicles only

d) Any vehicle

37. **When you are following a motorcyclist on the road with poor road surfaces. What should you do?**

a) Close up space so they can see you in their mirrors.

b) Overtake the motorcycle immediately to avoid delays.

c) Give extra room in case they turn sharply to avoid potholes.

d) Allow the same room and maintain the same speed.

38. **You need to check your tyres pressure regularly. How would you find the correct pressure to use when you want to put air into your tyres?**

a) It will be displayed on the tyre wall.

b) It will be written on the wheel.

c) By looking at the vehicle handbook.

d) By looking at the registration document.

39. **What does this sign mean?**

a)   A level crossing with gate or barrier ahead.

b)   Gated road ahead.

c)   Level crossing without gate or barrier ahead.

d)   Cattle grid ahead.

40. **You were driving and came to a motorway flooded with water, how are you going to ride through it?**

a)   Slowly, in a low gear

b)   Quickly, in a low gear

c)   Slowly, in a high gear

d)   Quickly, in a high gear

41. **When you see flashing amber lights under a school warning sign, you should:**

a)   Slow down until you are clear of the area

b)   Sound the horn and continue with the speed.

c)   Increase your speed and ride past the area quickly.

d)   Come to a stop and wait for the light to change to green.

42. **What does this sign mean?**

a) No services for 50 miles.

b) The temporary maximum speed required 50 mph.

c) Obstruction 50 metres ahead.

d) The temporary minimum speed required 50 mph.

43. **What should be your priority when you arrived at the scene of an accident and found someone unconscious?**

a) Check if their airway is clear.

b) Check for their name.

c) Wake them up.

d) Make them comfortable.

44. **Before riding anyone else's motorcycle, what should you be check?**

a) The owner's third-party insurance cover

b) Your motorcycle's insurance cover

c) If the motorcycle is insured for your use

d) If the owner has the insurance documents.

45. **What does a rumble device do?**

a) Keep cattle from escaping.

b) Inform you of low tyre pressure.

c) Alert you to a hazard.

d) Give directions

46. **You are driving on a one-way street and want to overtake a vehicle in front. Where may you overtake?**

a) Only on the right-hand side.

b) Overtaking isn't allowed.

c) Only on the left-hand side.

d) On either the left or right.

47. **Which of the following options is used to reduce traffic bunching on a road?**

a) Lane closures

b) Variable speed limits

c) Contraflow systems

d) National speed limits

48. **You're riding in the left-hand lane of a three-lane motorway. You observed that traffic is joining from a slip road. What should you do?**

a) Continue on your lane

b) Move to another lane

c) Keep a steady speed

d) Turn your hazard warning lights on

49. **Which one of the following is the effect of heavy braking and rapid acceleration?**

a) Increased road safety

b) Increased fuel consumption

c) Reduced pollution

d) Reduced exhaust emissions

50. On a wet road, a motorcyclist steers round drain covers on a bend. Why?

a) To prevent the tyres from puncturing on the edge of a drain cover.

b) To prevent the motorcycle from sliding on the metal drain covers.

c) To avoid hitting the pedestrian walking on the pavement.

d) To avoid splashing water on the pedestrians.

Answers To Theory Test 3

1	2	3	4	5	6	7	8	9	10
A	A	D	C	D	C	D	C	D	A

11	12	13	14	15	16	17	18	19	20
C	A	D	B	A	A	A	A	D	D

21	22	23	24	25	26	27	28	29	30
A	B	D	A	B	B	D	A	B	C

31	32	33	34	35	36	37	38	39	40
B	C	A	D	B	D	C	C	A	A

41	42	43	44	45	46	47	48	49	50
A	B	A	C	C	D	B	B	B	B

Chapter 4

Theory Test 4

1. **One of the factors that affect an elderly person's driving ability because:**

   a) They find it difficult to obtain car insurance.

   b) They'll require glasses to read road signs.

   c) They'll take a longer time to react to hazards.

   d) They will forget to signal at junctions.

2. **Which of the following must you obey when you are signal to STOP?**

   a) Motorcyclist

   b) Pedestrian

   c) Police officer

   d) Bus driver

3. **At the scene of a collision, you had a suspicion that one of the casualties has back injuries. And the area is safe, what should you do?**

   a) Offer them a drink

   b) Not move them

   c) Raise their legs

   d) Not call an ambulance

4. **You are riding on a motorway and your mobile phone rings. What should you do?**

   a) Stop immediately.

   b) Answer it immediately.

c) Ignore it and continue.

d) Pull up at the nearest kerb.

5. **What should you use the engine cut-out switch on your motorcycle to do?**

a) To stop the engine in an emergency.

b) To stop the engine on short journeys

c) To save wear on the ignition switch

d) To start the engine on the loss of key

6. **What precaution should you take when overtaking at night?**

a) Ride as you ride during the day.

b) Sound your horn loud before moving out

c) Make sure the headlights are on full beam

d) Watch out of bends in the road ahead

7. **When driving or riding along a motorway, you should:**

a) Try to look farther ahead than you would on other roads.

b) Ride faster than you would on other roads.

c) Keep a reduced separation distance than you would on other roads.

d) Increase your level of concentration than you would on other roads.

8. **You are travelling behind a long vehicle. There is a mini-roundabout in front. The vehicle is**

positioned to the right but signalling left. What should you do?

a) Sound your horn

b) Overtake on the left

c) Keep well back

d) Flash your headlights

9. **At the accident scene, someone is bleeding heavily from a wound sustained in the arm, and there is nothing embedded in the wound. How do you help that accident victim?**

a) Keep them talking

b) Dab the wound

c) Get them a drink

d) Apply pressure over the wound

10. **Which of the following conditions are you allowed to park on the right-hand side of a road at night?**

a) In a one-way street.

b) With your sidelights on.

c) Less than 10 metres (32 feet) from a junction.

d) Under a lamp-post.

11. **What does this sign mean?**

a) Give way to approaching vehicles.

b) Approaching vehicles can pass you on both sides.

c) Exit the next available junction.

d) Pass any of the sides to get to the same destination.

12. **You want to turn right while riding in a one-way street. There are two lanes. Which side of the lane would you position your vehicle?**

a) In the right-hand lane.

b) In the left-hand lane.

c) In either lane.

d) In the centre line.

13. **What does this sign mean?**

a) Cattle ranch ahead.

b) Museum ahead.

c) Humpback Bridge ahead.

d) Tunnel ahead.

14. **Which of the following do Diamond-shaped signs give instructions to?**

a) Tram drivers

b) Bus drivers

c) Lorry drivers

d) Taxi drivers

15. You are involved in an accident. What is the best thing to do to reduce the risk of fire?

a) Do not turn off the Engine.

b) Open the choke.

c) Turn the fuel tap to reserve.

d) Use the engine cut-out switch to turn off the bike.

16. What does this sign mean?

a) Waiting is not permitted.

b) Waiting permitted.

c) National speed limit permitted.

d) Parking is permitted.

17. **Someone suffered a burn following a collision. There is a need to cool the burn for some time. What is the shortest time?**

a) 5 minutes

b) 10 minutes

c) 15 minutes

d) 20 minutes

18. **What does this sign mean?**

a) Stopping is permitted only to pick up passengers.

b) Stopping is not permitted at any time.

c) Stopping is permitted only to set down passengers.

d) Stopping is not permitted at peak times.

19. **What does this traffic sign mean?**

a) Slippery road ahead.

b) Tyres service centre ahead.

c) Danger ahead.

d) Service area ahead.

20. **A bus is signaling to move away from a bus stop. And you are approaching the bus. What should you do?**

a) Increase your speed and ride pass immediately.

b) Allow the bus to move away if it is safe to do so.

c) Flash your headlights to show your presence.

d) Signals left and sound your horn.

21. **What does this sign mean?**

a) Pedestrians and cyclists are not permitted in this route.

b) Pedestrians route only.

c) Cyclists route only.

d) Pedestrians and cyclists route.

22. **What should you do when riding with a sidecar attached for the first time?**

a) Choose two answers.

b) Reduce your speed down

c) Be ready to stop more quickly

d) Increase your speed quickly round bends

e) Be careful on approach to corners

23. **You are approaching a busy junction with so many road markings on the lanes. What should you do when you notice that you are on the wrong lane at the last moment?**

a) Continue in that lane.

b) Force your way across.

c) Find your way and leave.

d) Signals to cut across.

24. **You plan to go abroad and will be driving on the right-hand side of the road. Which of the following would you fit in your motorcycle?**

a) Twin headlights.

b) Headlight deflectors.

c) Tinted yellow brake lights.

d) Tinted red indicator lenses.

25. **There is no traffic ahead, and you are riding at 70 mph on a three-lane motorway. Which of the following lane should you use?**

a) Any lane

b) Middle lane

c) Right-hand lane

d) Left-hand lane

26. **Which of the following situations are motorcyclists particularly vulnerable to?**

    a) When moving off.

    b) On dual carriageways.

    c) When approaching junctions.

    d) On motorway.

27. **Your motorcycle broke down on a motorway. You want to make an emergency call. How will you find the location of the nearest emergency telephone?**

    a) By following the flow of traffic.

    b) By following the arrow direction on a marker post.

    c) By moving against the flow of traffic.

    d) By sounding your horn.

28. **On what condition should you carry a child as a pillion passenger?**

    a) When the child is over 14 years old.

    b) When the child is over 16 years old.

    c) When the child can reach the floor from the seat.

    d) When the child can reach the handholds and. footrests.

29. **Where are reflective amber studs seen on a motorway?**

    a) In separating the slip road from the motorway.

b) On the far left-hand of the road.

c) On the far right-hand of the road.

d) Separating the lanes.

30. **In good road and weather conditions, what is the typical stopping distance at 70 mph?**

    a) 53 metres (175 feet)

    b) 60 metres (197 feet)

    c) 73 metres (240 feet)

    d) 96 metres (315 feet)

31. **You are riding at a legal speed limit, and a vehicle behind you is flashing its headlights. What should you do?**

    a) Signal the vehicle to slow down.

    b) Allow the vehicle to overtake you safely.

    c) Speed up and move away from the vehicle.

    d) Maintain your normal speed.

32. **There is a loose chipping warning ahead. What should be your next action?**

    a) Stop and look around.

    b) Accelerate and drive over them.

    c) Brake at the last moment.

    d) Slow down smoothly and safely.

33. **How often is the indicator on your motorcycle supposed to flash?**

    a) Between 7 to 8 times per second.

    b) Between 3 to 4 times per second.

c) Up to 2 times per second.

d) Between 5 to 6 times per second.

34. **In which of the following situation is overtaking not permitted?**

   a) When you are close to a dip.

   b) After you just got off from a bend.

   c) On a one way street.

   d) On the road with a speed limit of 30 mph.

35. **You are riding a motorcycle and your tyre gets punctured. What should you do?**

   a) Release the handlebars.

   b) Steer from side to side to regain your balance.

   c) Close the throttle and roll to a gentle stop.

   d) Perform an emergency stop.

36. **You are carrying a pillion passenger and want to ride around corners. What should the passenger do?**

   a) Lean with you.

   b) Lean against you.

   c) Signal for you.

   d) Look out for hazards.

37. **You rode through a flooded area of a road. What part of your motorcycle should you test when it is safe to do so?**

   a) The brakes

   b) The headlights

c) The starter meter

d) The steering.

38. **Which of the following is the best way to gain basic motorcycling skills?**

a) Ride round your street only on a dry day.

b) Ride on the motorway immediately.

c) Practice riding off-road under the supervision of an appropriate training body.

d) Practice off-road alone.

39. **It is mandatory for a motorcycle over three years old to have an MOT. Why?**

a) To show proof of ownership.

b) To allow for re-selling.

c) To show that it is roadworthy.

d) To show low fuel consumption.

40. **You are riding a motorcycle in a sunny condition, and you want to turn or change lane. What should you do?**

a) Flash your headlights before turning.

b) Give an arm signal as well as an indicator.

c) Sound your horn loud.

d) Position your hand firmly on the handlebars.

41. **A larger vehicle is moving in front of you, and you are keeping well back, planning to overtake it. Immediately a car overtakes you and fills the gap. What should be your reaction?**

a) Sound your horn very loud

b) Ignore the car and continue with your overtaking.

c) Flash your headlight angrily on the car

d) Drop further back.

42. **You are in a party where alcohol is freely available, and you intend to ride home afterward. What should you do?**

a) Drink up to the legal limit and stop

b) Drink below the legal limit

c) Avoid drinking any alcohol.

d) None of the above

43. **While riding on a motorway, you pass a car on the hard shoulder, showing a "Help" pennant. The driver of the car might be**

a) A new driver

b) A carriageway rescue officer

c) A first aider

d) Disabled

44. **The national speed limit for a motorcycle on a single carriageway is:**

a) 30 mph

b) 70mph

c) 50mph

d) 60mph

45. **You forgot to switch off the choke after the engine has warmed up. What will be the effect on your motorcycle?**

   a) Your braking distance will be cut short.

   b) Your battery will run down.

   c) The wear and tear of your engine will increase.

   d) There will be an increase in fuel consumption.

46. **The legal minimum insurance you must possess to ride your motorbike on public roads is:**

   a) Third-party, theft, and fire.

   b) Third-party.

   c) Personal injury cover.

   d) Comprehensive injury cover.

47. **If you want to carry a pillion passenger, which of these motorcycle components may have to be adjusted.**

   a) The brakes

   b) The indicators

   c) The Headlights

   d) The exhaust

48. **You are traveling through a tunnel in a jammed traffic. If you must stop, what action should you take?**

   a) Overlook the message signs in the tunnel

   b) Keep a good space from the vehicle in front of you.

c) Close up the gap by getting close to the vehicle in front

d) Do a U-turn and look for an exit.

49. **You should not wear one of the following while riding at night:**

a) A dark visor

b) Dark clothing

c) Sunglasses

d) All of the above

50. **How do signs giving orders which must be obeyed at all times look like?**

a) Blue squares

b) Brown triangles

c) Red triangles

d) Red circles

51. **What should you do when you are unexpectedly dazzled by the headlights of an approaching vehicle at night?**

a) Increase your speed and ride past the vehicle.

b) Slow down and be ready to stop.

c) Alert the driver by flashing your headlights.

d) Sound your horn and give an arm signal.

52. **On a motorway, which lane position should you choose when riding in normal conditions?**

a) Any lane is okay

b) The left of the lane

c) The centre of the lane

d) The far right of the lane

53. **What should you do anytime you are riding a motorcycle in windy conditions?**

a) Go low on speed.

b) Keep close to the gutter.

c) Ride close to a large vehicle.

d) Increase your speed

54. **One of the following vehicles is not permitted to drive on the motorway using the right-hand lane.**

a) A vehicle with a trailer.

b) A motorcycle

c) A motorcycle with a sidecar.

d) A delivery van

55. **What effect may towing a trailer behind your motorbike have?**

a) Your tyres grip on the road may increase.

b) Your motorcycle stopping distance may increase.

c) Your fuel consumption may reduce.

d) Handling may improve

56. **Overloading is a dangerous act. Whose duty is to make sure that the motorcycle is not overloaded?**

a) DVSA

b) The motorcycle's rider.

c) The owner of the load on the motorcycle.

d) The licensed owner of the motorcycle.

57. One of the tyre sidewalls of your vehicle tyres has a tear. What should you do?

a) Replace the tyre immediately.

b) Reduce the tyre pressure before you ride the motorcycle.

c) Ignore and continue riding.

d) Repair the punctured side before you ride the motorcycle.

58. The average braking distance of a motorcycle when riding at 50 mph on a good road surface in good conditions is:

a) 40 metres

b) 38 metres

c) 240 metres

d) 24 metres

59. A person involved in a collision can go into shock. Which of the following listed below is a sign of shock?

a) A flushed appearance.

b) Pale skin with a grey tinge.

c) A pulse below normal.

d) None of the above.

60. You are travelling in very cold weather and the looks wet. What should you do when you can't hear any sound from the road?

a) Keep throttling the engine to hear some sound.

b) Change into a lower gear.

c) Ignore and continue riding.

d) Reduce your speed and ride in a high gear.

Answers To Theory Test 4

1	2	3	4	5	6	7	8	9	10
C	C	B	C	A	D	A	C	D	A

11	12	13	14	15	16	17	18	19	20
D	A	D	A	D	A	B	B	C	B

21	22	23	24	25	26	27	28	29	30
D	A&D	A	B	D	C	B	D	C	D

31	32	33	34	35	36	37	38	39	40
B	D	C	A	C	A	A	C	C	B

41	42	43	44	45	46	47	48	49	50
D	C	D	D	C	B	C	B	D	D

51	52	53	54	55	56	57	58	59	60
B	C	A	A	B	B	A	B	B	D

Printed in Great Britain
by Amazon